My NAUGHTY Contact Lens

A fun
little rhyme
describing what
we love…
and what we
DON'T love…
about our
lenses!

Written by
Juliette Vignola

Illustrated by
Helen Dwiyanti

Inspired by
Samantha Vignola

My contact lens
   is my best friend!
   He helps me to see clearly.

But sometimes…
      every now and then…
he troubles me quite dearly!

Sometimes,
  when mom puts him in my eye,
    he won't go in.

He fights and fights,
  with all his might!
  But mom will <u>always</u> win!

Other times he's hanging out,
and quietly slips
out of place.

He floats around,
without a sound.
He might as well be in space!

There are days my lens gets dry
and he <u>really</u> needs a drop.

Mom helps me out
and drips it in,
and then the itching stops.

Once when I got pinkeye
    and I couldn't wear my lens,

I wore my glasses
        instead for a while
    but I sure did miss my friend!

Every now and then
my lens jumps right
out of my eye!

If I catch him in the act
I pick him up
so he won't get dry.

At times my lens gets dirty
and begins to scratch my eye.

My eye gets red,
it hurts my head!
To take him out we must try.

When mom tries
   to take out my lens,
   he sometimes gives her the slip.

We try and try,
   but he sticks in my eye!
   He has a very strong grip!

My lens sometimes gets dirty,
and it's difficult to see.

Mom cleans him up
and rubs him down
and everyone's happy!

Sometimes bad things happen,
and my lens gets a little rip.

When this happens,
(and it sometimes does)
to the garbage he gets a swift trip!

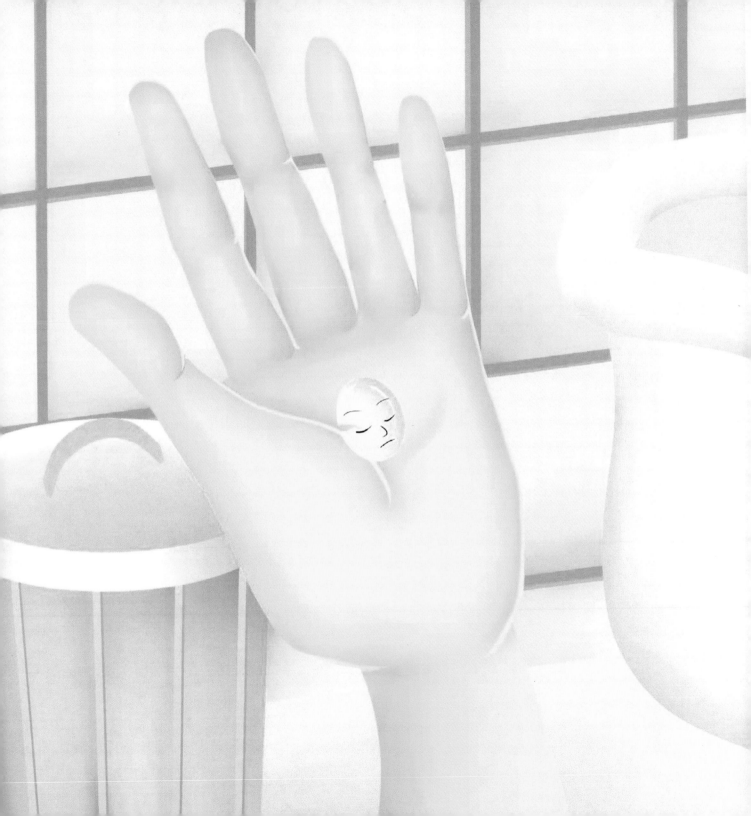

Eventually,
    each lens gets old,
    our time comes to an end.

I bid to him farewell,
        and mom brings in
            a brand new friend!

CONTACT LENS

I really love my contact,
though he sometimes
gives me pain.

He helps me see the best I can,
so I really can't complain!

Author's Notes

This book is dedicated to my most precious daughter Samantha. I would do anything to make the "contact lens" saga easier for you to handle, and this book is only one way I can try to help you and other children like you to try and make light of the difficulty contact lenses cause you. Some day you will realize how fortunate you are for your general health, and contact lenses will be no big deal to you. But right now, you're four years old and it is a big deal.
I love you, baby girl!

Please check out my other titles available on Amazon and Kindle worldwide:

Samantha Wears a Contact Lens and Patch... JUST LIKE YOU!
A day in the life of a unilateral aphakic child

Jack wears Contact Lenses and Glasses... JUST LIKE YOU!
A day in the Life of a bilateral aphakic child

Jack Wears Glasses and a Patch... JUST LIKE YOU!

Everyone's Different... JUST LIKE YOU! The Tale of Mango Sheep

This book is not intended as a substitute for the medical advice of a physician. The reader should regularly consult a physician in matters relating to his/her health or his/her child's health, and particularly with respect to any symptoms that may require diagnosis or medical attention.

Made in the USA
Lexington, KY
29 November 2015